JOBS IF YOU LIKE THE
CULINARY ARTS

by Marne Ventura

BrightP◆int Press

San Diego, CA

BrightPoint Press

© 2025 BrightPoint Press
an imprint of ReferencePoint Press, Inc.
Printed in the United States

For more information, contact:
BrightPoint Press
PO Box 27779
San Diego, CA 92198
www.BrightPointPress.com

LIBRARY OF CONGRESS CATALOGING-IN-PUBLICATION DATA

Names: Ventura, Marne, author.
Title: Jobs if you like the culinary arts / by Marne Ventura.
Description: San Diego, CA: BrightPoint Press, [2025] | Series: Job discovery | Includes
    bibliographical references and index. | Audience: Grades 7–9
Identifiers: LCCN 2024001076 (print) | LCCN 2024001077 (eBook) | ISBN 9781678209247
    (hardcover) | ISBN 9781678209254 (eBook)
Subjects: LCSH: Food service--Vocational guidance--Juvenile literature. | Cooks--Vocational
    guidance--Juvenile literature.
Classification: LCC TX911.3.V62 V46 2025 (print) | LCC TX911.3.V62 (eBook) | DDC
    641.5023--dc23/eng/20240126
LC record available at https://lccn.loc.gov/2024001076
LC eBook record available at https://lccn.loc.gov/2024001077

CONTENTS

THE CULINARY ARTS INDUSTRY AT
A GLANCE   4

INTRODUCTION   6
A SWEET JOB

CHAPTER ONE   10
PASTRY CHEF

CHAPTER TWO   22
CHEF

CHAPTER THREE   34
FOOD SERVICE MANAGER

CHAPTER FOUR   46
FOOD SCIENTIST OR TECHNOLOGIST

Other Jobs in the Culinary Arts Industry   58
Glossary   60
Source Notes   61
Index   62
Image Credits   63
About the Author   64

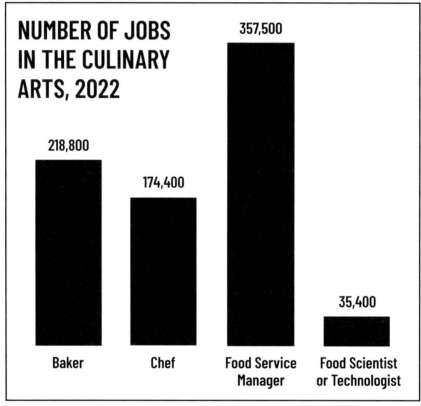

NUMBER OF JOBS IN THE CULINARY ARTS, 2022

- Baker: 218,800
- Chef: 174,400
- Food Service Manager: 357,500
- Food Scientist or Technologist: 35,400

Source: "Occupational Outlook Handbook," US Bureau of Labor Statistics, 2023. www.bls.gov.

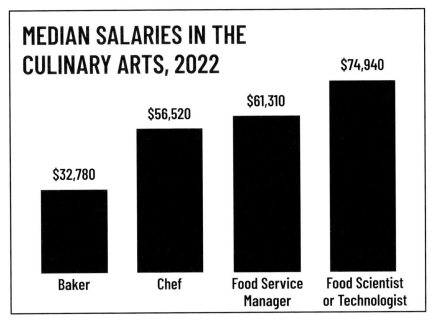

MEDIAN SALARIES IN THE CULINARY ARTS, 2022

$32,780	$56,520	$61,310	$74,940
Baker	Chef	Food Service Manager	Food Scientist or Technologist

Source: "Occupational Outlook Handbook," US Bureau of Labor Statistics, 2023. www.bls.gov.

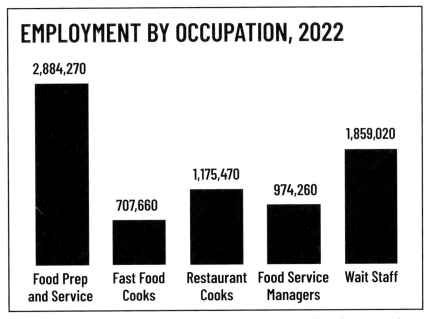

EMPLOYMENT BY OCCUPATION, 2022

2,884,270	707,660	1,175,470	974,260	1,859,020
Food Prep and Service	Fast Food Cooks	Restaurant Cooks	Food Service Managers	Wait Staff

Source: "Food Services and Drinking Places: Employment by Occupation," US Bureau of Labor Statistics, April 25, 2023. www.bls.gov.

A SWEET JOB

M ia works hard in a busy restaurant kitchen. She warms milk and melts chocolate. Then she mixes flour into the warm milk. Next, Mia pours this mixture over the chocolate. She whisks in egg yolks. She gently folds in whipped egg whites. Mia is a pastry chef. She is making **soufflé**. Next, Mia will scoop this batter into a **ramekin**. She will put it into the oven. As it bakes, it will rise above the edge of the baking dish.

Pastry chefs make many different desserts on any given day.

Pastry chefs are skilled at arranging ingredients in a pleasing way to decorate desserts.

"Our soufflés never leave our menu," says Mia. "That means this is something I do every single day. But I honestly love it. I think that soufflés are such a fun thing to have. It's really cool to me the way they work. I don't know, there's just something about them that I really, really like. So, I don't even mind that I have to do this every single day because it's so fun."[1]

Making soufflés is just one thing Mia does. Each day she puts on an apron.

Then she looks at her to-do list. She divides her baking tasks into steps. This is how she makes sure everything will be done on time. She does as many steps ahead of time as she can. She stays focused and keeps moving. When the restaurant closes, Mia scrubs her work areas and updates her to-do list for the next day.

WHAT ARE THE CULINARY ARTS?

Pastry chef is one of many careers options in the culinary arts industry. Everyone in the culinary arts works with food. Chefs create recipes. Food service managers run restaurants or dining halls. Food scientists study ways to create, package, and present food.

CHAPTER ONE

PASTRY CHEF

Pastry chefs are master bakers. They bake cakes, cookies, and pies. Some pastry chefs work in a bakery. These chefs bake breads and muffins. Others work in restaurants. They make up recipes for new desserts. Pastry chefs develop desserts that taste and look great.

Pastry chefs also work in hotels and resorts. They even work on cruise ships. Convention centers hire pastry chefs, too.

Pastry chefs add any finishing touches to baked goods just before they are placed in display cases.

Pastry Chef

Education: High school diploma or GED with 5 years of work experience or a certificate

Personal Qualities: Detail-oriented, good with hands, creative, a good team member, social, a good communicator, energetic

Certification and Licensing: Culinary Arts or Baking Pastry Certificate from a private school, or a 2-year degree in Baking and Pastry Arts from a community college

Working Conditions: Pastry chefs work in busy, crowded kitchens. They must work quickly and stay focused.

Average Salary: $66,792

Number of Jobs: 105,854

Future Job Outlook: 15 percent job growth from 2018 to 2028

Roland Mesnier was a pastry chef at the White House. He worked there for 26 years. He served five presidents. His mission was to make desserts to please the first family. They are always in the public eye. This can be stressful. Mesnier said, "If I could take away that pressure for 5 minutes, then I did my job. That was my role in the White House—to put a smile on the faces of the first family."[2]

TRAINING AND SKILLS

Pastry chefs need a high school diploma or **GED**. Private culinary arts programs offer 2- and 4-year options. Many community colleges offer 2-year degrees in pastry arts. Some 4-year colleges also offer these degrees. These programs teach students how to prepare desserts in the kitchen. Students learn how to take care of kitchen equipment. They also study nutrition and safe food storage. They learn how to plan a menu. Students study health and safety laws. They also learn how to manage **inventory**. Learning happens in the classroom and in the workplace.

Pastry chefs can also earn certificates in a specific area. Examples are baking **sanitation**, management, retail sales, and

Sweet or Savory

Culinary artists describe their creations as either sweet or savory. Savory dishes are the opposite of sweet. They taste spicy, salty, sour, or rich and meaty. Sweet dishes are often flavored with sugar, honey, or fruit.

Culinary school instructors guide students through the process of making different desserts, including cookies.

staff training. Retail Bakers of America is an industry association that offers many different certifications. The American Culinary Federation also offers special pastry chef certificates.

Pastry chefs are artists. They make desserts look beautiful. They need strong math and reading skills. This helps them

Some pastry chefs focus on making desserts that feature chocolate.

follow, adjust, and create recipes. Exact measurements are a must for baking success. Pastry chefs also need stamina. They work long hours. Chefs lift and carry heavy bags of ingredients. They should also be organized and be able to manage their time.

HOW TO GET STARTED

Hands-on practice in the kitchen is important. Aspiring pastry chefs should make candy, bread, and pastries. Reading cookbooks and watching baking shows are also good ways to learn the art. Some high schools offer baking classes. Working at a bakery, restaurant, or hotel can provide great experience.

Chefs' organizations offer pastry chef apprenticeship programs. The American Culinary Federation has programs across the United States. Students in these programs learn through classroom instruction. They also get on-the-job training. Sometimes the students are paid for their work. They are **mentored** by an experienced pastry chef.

British chef Gordon Ramsay has a television show called *MasterChef*. He has learned from pastry chefs throughout his career. Ramsay has trained many of the pastry chefs in his restaurants. He thinks mentoring is important. "If you want to

Working with a pastry chef who has years of experience is a great way to learn how to bake bread and pastries.

become a great chef, you have to work with great chefs," he says. "And that's exactly what I did."[3]

FUTURE DIRECTIONS

The US Bureau of Labor Statistics (BLS) gathers information about different careers. It estimates a 15 percent growth in jobs for pastry chefs and bakers from 2018 to 2028. It predicts that more bakers will be needed in places that make and sell baked goods.

New laws passed in the 2010s made it less costly for pastry chefs to start their own businesses. The laws allow chefs and bakers to make breads and pastries in their home kitchens. This allows pastry chefs who might not be able to open a bakery to run their own businesses. They may

Home businesses allow pastry chefs to bake without the costs of renting a commercial kitchen.

make and sell artisan breads. Others might decorate wedding cakes.

The COVID-19 pandemic pushed more pastry chefs to start their own businesses. Some began baking bread at home. Many promoted their pastries and breads on social media. They sold baked goods to neighbors. Others got booths at their local farmers markets.

FIND OUT MORE

The Bread Bakers Guild of America
www.bbga.org
The Bread Bakers Guild of America is an organization for professional bakers, farmers, educators, and bakery owners. It offers educational resources for bread making.

The Retail Bakers of America
www.retailbakersofamerica.org
The Retail Bakers of America is an organization that provides support, resources, and networking opportunities. It also helps bakers keep up with the latest trends in the industry.

CHAPTER TWO

CHEF

C hefs are the highest-ranking workers in a kitchen. They decide how to prepare and serve the food. Executive chefs oversee the kitchen staff. They decide which foods to include on the menu.

Chefs work in many settings. They might be head cooks in small local restaurants. Sometimes they supervise staff in a large chain restaurant. Chefs work for catering companies. These businesses make food

Chefs may cook or direct other chefs to make the dishes featured on the menu.

Chef

Minimum Education: High school diploma or GED; culinary program at a community college, private school, or 4-year college; 5 years of work experience

Personal Qualities: Good at food preparation, dedicated to customer service, a good business manager, creative in making and presenting recipes

Certification and Licensing: Private culinary schools offer specialized certificates for sous chef, executive chef, or private chef

Working Conditions: Chefs work in restaurants, hotels, schools, and other places where food is prepared and served. They often work early mornings, late evenings, weekends, and holidays. The work atmosphere is usually very busy.

Salary: $56,520

Number of Jobs: 174,400

Future Job Outlook: 5 percent job growth from 2022 to 2032

for events such as weddings or parties. Cruise ships hire chefs to prepare food for travelers.

Chefs can also cook for those in need. For example, Chef José Andrés helps people around the world. After the 2010 earthquake in Haiti, he founded the World

Some chefs may chop ingredients while others make meals.

Central Kitchen. It prepares and delivers fresh meals to people affected by disasters. Andrés is passionate about feeding others. He says, "The business of feeding people is the most amazing business in the world."[4]

Students practice their cooking skills during hands-on classes offered at culinary schools.

TRAINING AND SKILLS

Chefs need a high school diploma or GED. Community colleges and private schools offer 2-year culinary arts degrees. Four-year culinary arts degrees are offered at some colleges and universities. The Culinary Institute of America (CIA) is a well-known school. It was founded in 1946. It offers classes in baking and management. The CIA also teaches about the science of food. Hands-on training is part of the program.

Chefs need a mix of skills. They are experts at making tasty dishes. They create recipes. They arrange food so it looks good on the plate. Chefs also make sure their ingredients are fresh. They know how much food to order and keep in stock. James Beard is an American chef and cookbook author. He stresses the importance of starting with fresh ingredients. He says, "There is absolutely no substitute for the best. Good food cannot be made of inferior ingredients masked with high flavor."[5]

Chefs are also good team leaders. They make sure their **sous chef** and cooks prepare the food correctly. Chefs teach staff

Chef or Cook?

Chefs and cooks have different roles. Chefs have years of training. They are managers who are experts at running the kitchen. They decide what foods to make and how to make them. Cooks are skilled at preparing certain foods. They perform day-to-day tasks in the kitchen. Cooks prepare the food under the direction of the chef.

to follow food safety and sanitation rules. They train kitchen staff. Chefs inspire them to create delicious meals. Daniel Boulud is a successful French chef. He explains, "To me, there's no great chef without a great team."[6]

HOW TO GET STARTED

Would-be chefs can practice their cooking skills at home. There are many books, videos, and television programs for learning to cook. Some high schools offer cooking classes. Business and math classes can be helpful as well. Working in a restaurant or other food service business is one way to get started. Summer jobs may be offered through restaurants or catering companies.

Other options are summer camps, hospitals, or schools.

Chef apprenticeship programs assign students to a working kitchen. It could be a restaurant or an assisted living community. These programs are offered through professional organizations. One example is the American Culinary Federation.

FUTURE DIRECTIONS

The BLS predicts that jobs for chefs will grow by 5 percent between 2022 and 2032. It also estimates that the average income for chefs will rise in that period. According to BLS, overall growth in income will drive people to eat out more often.

There is a rising interest in healthy, delicious meals beyond what is served in

Food trucks offer another business opportunity for chefs. Trucks can move where customers are enjoying outdoor events and activities.

sit-down restaurants. The US food truck industry has grown by almost 10 percent between 2018 and 2023. Chefs create the menus and make the food sold from trucks. The trucks travel to different locations and serve food.

Diners want high-quality dishes. They like to order foods that they aren't likely to make at home. Restaurants will need to hire chefs to meet this increased demand.

FIND OUT MORE

American Culinary Federation

www.acfchefs.org

The American Culinary Federation provides information about the latest industry trends. It also offers educational opportunities to food professionals. These include certificate and apprenticeship programs.

The American Institute of Wine & Food

www.aiwf.org

The American Institute of Wine & Food offers educational programs. One pairs fourth- and fifth-grade students with local chefs who teach them about cooking.

National Restaurant Association

www.restaurant.org

The National Restaurant Association has an online learning center. It provides information on restaurant business practices, food, and menu trends. It also has podcasts featuring stories about the restaurant business.

CHAPTER THREE

FOOD SERVICE MANAGER

F ood service managers run businesses where food is made and served. Some manage family-owned restaurants. Others run big chain restaurants or hotel restaurants. Some oversee cafeterias in schools, factories, or office buildings.

Those who enjoy food and like working with people make good food service managers. They make sure their staff are trained and motivated. Their goal is to

Food service managers may run small coffee shops, bakeries, restaurants, or cafeterias.

make sure their customers have a good experience. Dave Thomas founded the Wendy's restaurant chain. When he was 8,

Food Service Manager

Education: High school diploma or equivalent with on-the-job training or a 2- or 4-year degree in food service management

Personal Qualities: Energetic, social, a motivator, a good manager

Certification and Licensing: Some states require a food safety certificate and license

Working Conditions: Schedules often include nights, weekends, and holidays. Work is fast-paced and intense.

Average Salary: $61,310

Number of Jobs: 357,500

Future Job Outlook: 0 percent job growth from 2022 to 2032

Since the opening of the first Wendy's in Columbus, Ohio, in 1969, many locations have opened across the country.

he dreamed of running a restaurant. He made his dream come true. Dave Thomas loved food and people. He says, "It all comes back to the basics. Serve customers the best-tasting food at a good value in a clean, comfortable restaurant, and they'll keep coming back."[7]

TRAINING AND SKILLS

Food service managers need a high school diploma or GED. Some managers may start as servers or cooks. Then they work their way up. But many go to college. Public and private colleges offer 2- and 4-year college degrees in hospitality or food service management.

Food service managers need a wide range of skills. They hire, train, and

Front and Back of House

In food and hospitality jobs, workers are organized into two groups. Front of house workers interact with the guests often. They include servers and restaurant managers. Back of house workers spend most of their days behind the scenes. Chefs and pastry chefs are back of house jobs.

Managers meet with head chefs to discuss any changes that need to be made to the menu.

supervise staff members. When problems arise, they find a solution. For example, if food isn't being served quickly enough, they figure out what is causing the slow service. Then they make a new plan to speed up the process. Food service managers decide staff schedules. They need to know

Working in a restaurant can be a good way to get food service experience.

labor laws. Managers must have just the right number of staff. Too many workers can cost the business too much money in salaries. Not enough workers can lead to poor customer service.

Food service managers understand budgets. A business makes a profit by taking in more money than it spends. Food service managers know how to order the correct amounts of supplies. They minimize food waste. But they must make sure the business always has what it needs to serve its customers.

HOW TO GET STARTED

After-school and summer jobs in food service are valuable ways to gain experience. Volunteering to work at organizations where food is prepared and served is also an option. Examples may be churches, shelters, or summer camps. Food service managers need good leadership skills. Sports teams, student government, or clubs offer opportunities to learn to lead.

Earning a certificate is another way to build skills. State or local health departments offer food safety certificates.

Managers can order food and track inventory using the latest software for food service businesses.

Students who pass a food safety exam can earn food protection manager certification. Employers like to see this certification. Some states have apprenticeship programs. They provide a way for people with no experience or formal training to get a start in the industry.

FUTURE DIRECTIONS

The BLS predicts the number of food service manager jobs from 2022 to 2032 will remain the same. Despite the slow growth, the BLS estimates about 39,600 job openings each year. These openings are due to workers moving to different jobs or retiring. One reason for slow job growth may be that more restaurants are having chefs manage the restaurant. This saves the business money on staff.

Technology is also changing food service management. For example, many restaurants now use mobile ordering apps. A staff person used to serve customers. But now customers can place their order before they arrive. Computer systems can track inventory as food is sold. This means managers spend less time figuring out what foods to order. These new technologies can make the job of a food service manager easier.

FIND OUT MORE

The Association of Nutrition & Foodservice Professionals

www.anfponline.org

The Association of Nutrition & Foodservice Professionals offers education and resources for food service managers. It hosts conferences and awards ceremonies.

Society for Hospitality and Food Service Management

www.shfm-online.org

The Society of Hospitality and Food Service Management puts on conferences throughout the year. Professionals can network and learn about current trends in the industry.

CHAPTER FOUR

FOOD SCIENTIST OR TECHNOLOGIST

Food scientists study how to improve foods. They find new ways to farm and prepare food. They study ways to keep food fresh. Food scientists study foods to learn how nutritious they are. They use skills in chemistry, microbiology, and other sciences. They learn better ways to produce and deliver food to people. Food scientists do research in labs or on farms. Others work in offices. They study **food policy**.

Food scientists study foods such as tomatoes to learn how they can make the fruit more resistant to diseases.

Food Scientist or Technologist

Education: 4-year college degree; sometimes a master's degree

Personal Qualities: Strong in math and science, a problem-solver, analytical, interested in food production or agriculture

Certification and Licensing: Certified Food Scientist (CFS), Certified Food Safety Scientist, Agricultural Consultant

Working Conditions: Food scientists work at a computer, travel to inspect food processing plants, or analyze food in a lab at a private company, university, or government agency.

Average Salary: $74,940

Number of Jobs: 35,400

Future Job Outlook: 6 percent job growth from 2022 to 2032

Food technologists use science to find the best ways to create, package, and preserve processed foods. These are foods that have been altered during preparation. Processing can be freezing, canning, cooking, or drying. Examples include breakfast cereals, canned vegetables, or microwavable meals. Food technologists often work for big companies that make processed foods.

TRAINING AND SKILLS

Food scientists and technologists need 4-year college degrees. They may major in food science, food technology, or food engineering. Others may study chemistry, biology, or engineering. Agriculture or business degrees are sometimes accepted as well.

A strong knowledge of biology and chemistry is a must for these jobs. Students learn how processed foods are made. They also study how to distribute those products. Food scientists need good English and communication skills. And they must be skilled with technology. This helps them analyze data and report their findings.

Food for the Future

Food scientists are studying new ways to produce food. They want to find ways to grow food without harming the environment. These methods avoid chemicals. They use less energy and reuse resources. One example of this is aquaponics. This is a system that recycles the water used to produce food.

Chemistry and biology classes provide a strong foundation for students interested in food science.

HOW TO GET STARTED

Students should take a lot of math, science, and English classes in high school. They should also learn computer software.

Students learn how to conduct experiments on plants and analyze the results.

Programs for creating spreadsheets and presentations are especially important.

Colleges with strong food science or technology programs are a good choice. Students learn physics, biochemistry, math, and microbiology. They also take classes in social sciences, humanities, and business. Food chemistry, food analysis, and nutrition classes are part of their studies.

Students often complete an internship as well. Private companies such as the Hershey Company offer internships. This company makes chocolate and other candies. Students practice designing and managing ways to produce food. They evaluate data, write reports, and present results.

FUTURE DIRECTIONS

The BLS predicts 6 percent job growth for food science and technology from 2022 to 2032. New research is constantly published about healthy diets. This creates a demand for new and improved processed foods.

This is where food scientists can help. For example, food scientist Rebeca Lopez-Garcia helped a coffee grower in Ecuador. She found ways to keep coffee fresh and safe during shipping. She also worked with the governments of Egypt and Panama. She helped them increase profits for their food growers.

Lopez-Garcia likes the variety in her work. She says, "People always have to eat, so it is a very stable industry, and it gives you a great sense of purpose since nutrition

Studies about what makes up a nutritious diet have led to a greater demand for healthy foods.

Food scientists work to bring the healthiest foods to dinner tables around the world.

is essential for good health. In addition, food and eating are very social, so your work is present in everybody's family events. You can really make a difference in this area."[8]

For those who love food, the culinary arts industry provides many career paths. Pastry chefs and chefs prepare foods. Food service managers like to work with people. And food scientists find ways to improve food nutrition and production.

FIND OUT MORE

Association for Women in Science
www.awis.org
Association for Women in Science provides support and information to women seeking careers in science. It also posts a variety of jobs available in food science.

Cereals & Grains Association
www.cerealsgrains.org
The Cereals and Grains Association is a global organization of scientists and food industry professionals. It offers information about research, education, and leadership.

Institute of Food Technologists
www.ift.org
The Institute of Food Technologists provides industry news. It also sponsors events where members can network and post job openings.

OTHER JOBS IN THE CULINARY ARTS INDUSTRY

Nutritionist

Nutritionists plan and manage food programs to help people lead healthy lives. They might work in hospitals, nursing homes, medical clinics, or cafeterias. Nutritionists earn 4-year college degrees and get hands-on training through internships. They learn the dietary needs of their clients and design food plans. They also counsel and educate clients on healthy eating habits.

Caterer

Caterers prepare food for events. These may include weddings, parties, and business meetings. Some work directly with clients to create a menu. They also set up food at the event location and clean up afterward. Caterers must know and follow laws related to health and safety laws. They may be self-employed, or they may work for a catering company.

Food Stylist

Food stylists arrange food
before it is photographed
or filmed. These photos or
videos are used in cookbooks,
magazines, advertisements,
menus, or television shows.
Food stylists learn tricks to

make food look delicious. For example, they paint shiny glazes
on cakes. Sometimes they use nonfood items. For example,
motor oil is often used instead of syrup because it looks better
in photos. Food stylists need at least a 2-year degree from a
culinary arts school.

Food Writer

Food writers work for
magazines, newspapers,
and book publishers. They
may also work for radio and
television stations. They report
about food or cooking events
and interview chefs or other

experts in the culinary arts. They write reviews of recipes
and restaurants. Food writers typically have 4-year degrees
in English or journalism. They have excellent communication
skills. They are knowledgeable about food and they
are creative.

GLOSSARY

food policy

a plan for how food is produced, processed, distributed, and purchased

GED

a test students take that is equivalent to earning a high school diploma

inventory

all of the goods and materials on hand

mentored

to be taught a trade or skill

ramekin

a single-serving baking dish

sanitation

the process of making things clean

soufflé

a dish made from eggs and other ingredients that puffs up when baked

sous chef

the top assistant to the head chef

SOURCE NOTES

INTRODUCTION: A SWEET JOB

1. Quoted in "Day in My Life as a Pastry Chef 2021: Boston," *YouTube*, uploaded by Mia Bakes, March 23, 2021. www.youtube.com.

CHAPTER ONE: PASTRY CHEF

2. Quoted in "An Homage to White House Pastry Chef Roland Mesnier," *Collin Street Bakery*, October 5, 2022. www.collinstreet.com.

3. Quoted in Chris Hill, "20 Quotes from Successful Chefs: What They've Learned from a Career in the Kitchen," *Medium*, December 17, 2015. www.medium.com.

CHAPTER TWO: CHEF

4. Quoted in "21 Best Chef José Andrés Quotes About Food, Life, and Purpose," *GoodGoodGood*, January 18, 2023. www.goodgoodgood.com.

5. Quoted in "6 James Beard Quotes Sure to Inspire Your Culinary Arts Career," *ECPI University*, n.d. www.ecpi.edu.

6. Quoted in "The Chef's Supporting Cast," *Santé Magazine*, March 1, 2023. www.santemagazine.com.

CHAPTER THREE: FOOD SERVICE MANAGER

7. Quoted in "Dave Thomas Quotes," *BrainyQuote*, n.d. www.brainyquote.com.

CHAPTER FOUR: FOOD SCIENTIST OR TECHNOLOGIST

8. Quoted in "An Interview with a Food Scientist," *i-STUDENTglobal*, n.d. www.i-studentglobal.com.

INDEX

American Culinary Federation, 15, 17, 30, 33

Andrés, José, 25–26

apprenticeship programs, 17, 30, 33, 43

Beard, James, 27–28

Boulud, Daniel, 29

catering companies, 22, 29

certificates, 12, 14–15, 24, 33, 36, 42–43, 48

chefs, 9, 22–33, 38, 43

cooks, 22, 28, 38

culinary arts programs, 13, 24, 27

Culinary Institute of America, 27

culinary schools, 24

executive chefs, 22, 24

food engineering, 49

food policy, 46

food scientists, 9, 46–57

food service businesses, 29, 34, 41

food service managers, 9, 34–45, 38

food technology, 49

food truck industry, 30–32

GED, 12, 13, 24, 27, 38

home businesses, 19–20

internships, 53

job growth, 12, 19, 24, 30, 36, 43, 48, 54

Lopez-Garcia, Rebeca, 54, 56

MasterChef, 18

mentoring, 17, 18–19

Mesnier, Roland, 13

nutrition, 14, 45, 46, 53, 54

pastry chefs, 6–9, 10–21, 38

processed foods, 49–50, 54

Ramsay, Gordon, 18–19

Retail Bakers of America, 15, 21

salaries, 12, 24, 36, 48

schedule, 16, 36, 39

skills, 13, 15–16, 27, 29, 38–41, 42, 46, 48, 49–50

social media promotion, 20

sous chefs, 24, 28

technology, 44, 49, 50, 53, 54

Thomas, Dave, 36–37

work experience, 17, 24, 41, 43

World Central Kitchen, 25–26

IMAGE CREDITS

Cover: © Dean Drobot/Shutterstock Images
4: © Red Line Editorial
5: © Red Line Editorial
7: © Studio Peace/Shutterstock Images
8: © CandyRetriever/Shutterstock Images
11: © El Greco 1973/Shutterstock Images
15: © Roman Seliutin/Shutterstock Images
16: © JG Fotografia/Shutterstock Images
18: © David Fuentes Prieto/Shutterstock Images
20: © Odua Images/Shutterstock Images
23: © wavebreakmedia/Shutterstock Images
25: © Gorodenkoff/Shutterstock Images
26: © Party People Studio/Shutterstock Images
31: © Blulz60/Shutterstock Images
35: © PeopleImages.com-Yuri A./Shutterstock Images
37: © Tada Images/Shutterstock Images
39: © WBMUL/Shutterstock Images
40: © Monkey Business Images/Shutterstock Images
42: © baranq/Shutterstock Images
47: © wavebreakmedia/Shutterstock Images
51: © aslysun/Shutterstock Images
52: © MNBB Studio/Shutterstock Images
55: © Aleksandar Malivuk/Shutterstock Images
56: © Monkey Business Images/Shutterstock Images
58 (top): © Prostock-Studio/Shutterstock Images
58 (bottom): © Halfpoint/Shutterstock Images
59 (top): © Pressmaster/Shutterstock Images
59 (bottom): © Gorodenkoff/Shutterstock Images

ABOUT THE AUTHOR

Marne Ventura is the author of more than one hundred books for children. A former elementary teacher, she holds a master's degree in reading and language development from the University of California. Marne's nonfiction titles cover a wide range of topics, including careers, STEM, arts and crafts, food and cooking, health, and survival. Her fiction series, The Worry Warriors, tells the story of four brave kids who learn to conquer their fears. Marne and her family live in California.